TALES OF HORROR

GHOSTS

Jim Pipe

ticktock

TALES OF HORROR
GHOSTS

Acknowledgements

Copyright © 2006 *ticktock* Entertainment Ltd.

First published in Great Britain by ticktock Media Ltd.,

Unit 2, Orchard Business Centre, North Farm Road, Tunbridge Wells, Kent TN2 3XF, Great Britain.

A CIP catalogue record for this book is available from the British Library.

ISBN 1 84696 014 2 Printed in China.

Picture Credits

t=top, b=bottom, c=centre, l=left, r=right, OFC=outside front cover, OBC=outside back cover.

Amit Gogia CyberMedia Services: 28-29 (main pic). Corbis: 25br. Fortean Picture Library: 9cr, 10bc. Image Select: 30tl. c.Paramount/Everett/Rex Features 5cr. ShutterStock: 1, 4/5 (main pic), 6tl, 10/11 (main pic), 16/17 (main pic), 22/23 (main pic), 26/27 (main pic), Mehmet Alci 8bl, Gilles DeCruyenaere 8/9 (main pic), Denisenko 4bl, Chris Harvey 6/7 (main pic), Sarah Johnson 6cb, CVP 18/19 (main pic), Nathan B Dappen 30/31 (main pic), Chris Harvey 18tl, Craig Hosterman 14cb, Barbara Jablonska 31tr, Pam Kane 22tl, Raymond Kasprzak 19bl, Jimmy Lee 24bl, Patricia Malina 14tl, Michael Marquand 26tl, Thomas Nord 27tr, Kevin Norris 23tl, Vladimír Radosa 12/13 (main pic), Clive Watkins 14/15 (main pic), Neil Webster 13cr, Darren Wiseman 24/25 (main pic). ticktock Media image archive 10tl, 12bl, 18tl, 20bl, 27tr, 28bl.

Every effort has been made to trace the copyright holders and we apologize in advance for any unintentional ommissions.

We would be pleased to insert the appropriate acknowledgement in any subsequent edition of this publication.

CONTENTS

WELCOME TO THE SPIRIT WORLD

Tap, tap. In the dead of night, a sound wakes you. Tap, tap. A dark shape appears at the window. Is that a branch blowing in the wind? Or could it be – a ghost!

Be afraid, be very afraid! If you believe the stories, ghosts are all around us. When someone says the word 'ghost', do you imagine a creepy old mansion on a dark, stormy night? Think again. Ghosts can appear anywhere, any time!

Ghosts can walk through walls and even through living people. Ghosts can be a horrible face at the window, a phantom ship floating above the sea or a bright ball of light. Ghosts are said to be restless souls that cannot find peace in death. Some want a proper burial, others want revenge on their killers. If you are lucky, they may ignore you.

Sometimes ghosts do not appear. But they let us know they are there, by moving objects or making strange noises. That icy shudder down your spine could be a ghost walking past…

FRIEND OR FOE?

Ghosts have been giving people goosebumps for centuries. Usually they do not harm the person who sees them. Some good ghosts try to warn strangers of danger. Others attach themselves to children and try to become their friend!

Be warned, however. Some stories tell of less friendly, or evil-minded ghosts. These evil spooks play tricks on people, and push them around. But can we believe such tales? Read on and make up your own mind!

"Ichabod was horror-struck on perceiving that he was headless! But his horror was still more increased on observing that the head, which should have rested on his shoulders, was carried before him on the pommel of his saddle!"

From *The Legend of Sleepy Hollow* (1820) by Washington Irving.

RESTLESS SOULS

What is a ghost? Is it the soul of someone who has died? Or a force of nature we do not understand? Or do ghosts only exist in our minds?

HOLY GHOSTS

Most graveyards are said to have a ghost. In ancient times a living person could be killed to become a graveyard guardian. It was thought that their good spirit would protect the graveyard from evil ones.

The ghosts of priests or nuns haunt churches all over the world. The 'Grey Lady' is a nun who haunts the site of a hospital in York. She fell in love with a young nobleman. When the lovers were found out, the nun was thrown into a windowless room. This was then bricked up to make a living tomb!

NIGHT AND DAY

In Europe, more people claim to see ghosts at Halloween than any other night.

People are afraid of seeing ghosts at night, but most are spotted during the day.

A ghost is often thought to be the spirit, or soul, of a person who has stayed on Earth after death. They might stay to warn a loved one about some danger. Or, they might want to take revenge on a person who harmed them. Ghosts appear all over the world, but people disagree about what they are and how they behave.

In some parts of the world, such as China, people believe that when we die our souls can enter somebody else's body. However, some ghost hunters believe ghosts are just energy left over when people die. So they hunt for ghosts using electrical detectors.

LOOKING SPOOKY

Whooooooohh! When you think of a ghost, do you imagine a figure floating around in a white sheet, moaning and dragging clanking chains behind it?

Ghosts do not have solid bodies like living people. People often describe them as being 'silvery' or 'shadowy'. Many ghosts appear in the clothes they wore when they died. In 1953, ghostly Roman soldiers marched through a house in York, England. They wore battle clothes and carried spears. Some ghosts drag chains behind them, a sign that they were criminals.

Many famous ghosts carry their heads under their arm. This is usually because they had their heads cut off. Other headless horsemen ride black horses and carry their heads on their saddles. Some of the spookiest ghosts are those without eyes. When you look at their face, two black sockets stare back at you!

"At this the spirit raised a frightful cry, and shook its chain with such a dismal and appalling noise, that Scrooge held on tight to his chair, to save himself from falling in a swoon."

From *A Christmas Carol* (1843) by Charles Dickens.

HAUNTED HOUSES

It is a wild and stormy night. Lightning flashes and you see a ruined castle in the distance. You need shelter but is this terrible place haunted? Do you dare enter?

Anywhere people have lived can be haunted. This includes inns, schools, theatres and railway stations. Since 1550, a spooky cry has been heard in the streets of Mexico City at midnight. It belongs to the 'wailing woman' who was hanged for murdering her children.

Many old castles have their own ghost. The 'White Lady' walks the battlements of Rochester Castle in Kent. Places where people have been executed are also often haunted. Ghosts at the Tower of London include two murdered princes, and a group of ghostly guards chasing Lady Salisbury – with an axe!

THE MOST HAUNTED HOUSE?

Ghost-hunter Harry Price investigated Borley Rectory in the 1930s. Harry found this mysterious writing on the walls. He also recorded unexplained footsteps, ringing doorbells, smashed glasses, stone throwing and people being thrown from their beds!

The rectory has been called 'the most haunted house in England'. It's easy to understand why!

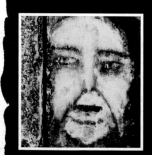

THE HOUSE OF THE FACES

On 23rd August, 1971, Maria Pereira caught sight of a mark on her kitchen floor. She tried to scrub it off, but it grew bigger. It started to look like a face. The floor was re-laid. Then the face appeared again!

Over the years, different faces appeared and disappeared. Finally the floor was ripped up again. This time workmen found a graveyard. The skeletons were removed and a new floor put down. But the faces kept coming back!

WHO'S THERE?

You hear footsteps, see a fork flying through the air and a strange smell fills the room. The hairs on the back of your neck stand up. But, you can't see anything...

We use the word 'ghost' to describe all sorts of strange things that we can't explain. Do you ever feel that something is watching you, even though you can't see it? Or, does part of a room sometimes feel very cold for no reason?

Ghosts get in touch with the living in different ways. They can spook animals, blow out candles or make objects suddenly disappear and reappear again. Some ghosts let us know they are there with strange smells. The ghosts that haunt Cotehele House in Cornwall, England, sometimes fill rooms with a strong smell of herbs!

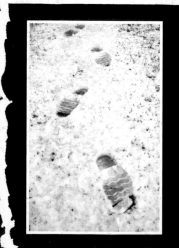

THINGS THAT GO BUMP IN THE NIGHT

Some ghosts appear to leave behind traces. These can be footprints in the dust, soil or food. Others touch or stroke the living. More annoying ghosts throw objects, move pictures, write on walls and slam doors.

Ghosts also create all kinds of unusual sounds, such as footsteps, knocking, scratching, whispering or bell-ringing. Other ghosts shriek and moan. Banshees are Irish ghosts with a scream so sharp it can shatter glass!

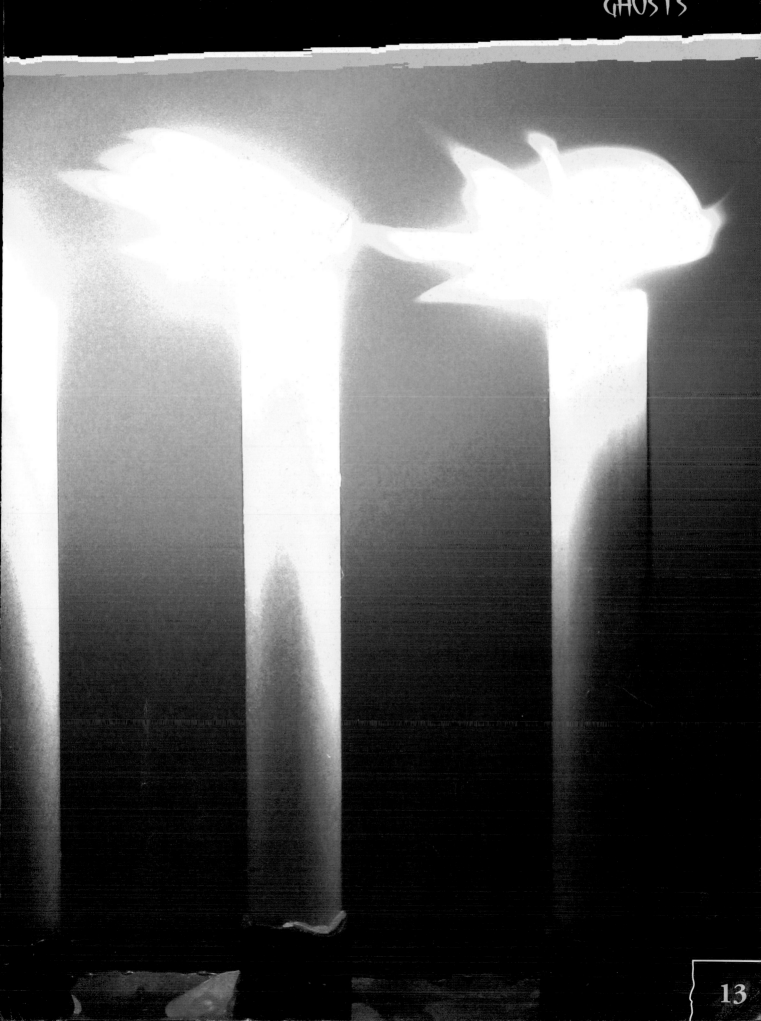

POLTERGEISTS

RASH! A plate flies across the room and smashes into the wall. You turn around, but no one is there. Then another plate rises into the air. What is happening?

The German word poltergeist means 'noisy ghost'. Poltergeists often attach themselves to a single place or person. Between 1925-27 poltergeists picked on Romanian, Eleonore Zügun, in three different houses. Stones were thrown at her house by invisible powers. Also, strange forces slapped and scratched her face.

A poltergeist likes making mischief and upsetting people. Poltergeists can make objects or even people rise into the air. They also light fires, blow winds through a house, move chairs or slam doors. Having a poltergeist in your house can be a real nuisance, and scary!

THE JOLLER POLTERGEIST

In the 1860s a famous poltergeist pestered the Joller Family. They lived near Lake Lucerne in Switzerland. The poltergeist kept waking them up with knocking noises.

One day the knocking became so loud that the family fled. When the Jollers moved back in, the poltergeist began moving furniture, slamming doors and starting fires.

Another time, an apple mysteriously hopped around the house. A servant threw the apple out of the window, but it came flying back in!

TIDY GHOST

In Russian folklore, a 'domovoy' is a household spirit. It looks like a tiny old man with a face covered in white fur. If you don't look after your home, it tickles you as you sleep, knocks on the wall and throws pans and plates.

GHOSTBUSTING

Do doors slam on their own? Are knocking sounds keeping you awake? Do pictures keep moving by themselves? It's time to call the ghostbusters!

Most people do not believe in ghosts. All the same, large numbers of ghosts are reported every year. Many people take these sightings seriously and investigate them.

The Ghost Club Society of Great Britain was set up in 1862. It was the first organisation to discuss and record ghosts. It also investigates other strange events, known as the 'paranormal'.

Early ghost hunters used candles to pick up ghostly breezes. They also sprinkled chalk or flour on surfaces to find ghostly prints.

Today's ghost hunters use hi-tech equipment. Laptop computers are linked to sensors that start automatic cameras to catch ghosts on video. Sensitive thermometers pick up sudden changes in temperature.

ECTOPLASM

Some ghosts leave behind a horrible sticky mucus called ectoplasm. Ghost hunters say this is what ghosts are made of.

In the early 20th century, ghost hunter and magician Harry Houdini found that most ectoplasm was fake. People blew cotton mixed with goose fat or chewed bits of paper from their mouths. They then called it ectoplasm.

GHOSTLY HABITS

Ghosts have all sorts of unusual habits, just like us! Some ghosts appear just once. Others keep returning to the same place.

The headless ghost of Anne Boleyn haunts eight different places in England. Perhaps she is still angry at her husband King Henry VIII, who had her beheaded in 1536.

GHOSTLY FOLK

A car drives along a road. Suddenly, a hitch-hiker appears at the roadside. The car stops, the hitch-hiker climbs in. Then he vanishes!

Phantom hitch-hikers appear in many ghost stories. Often the ghost asks the driver to give them a lift – to the graveyard where they are buried!

Other ghostly folk include gallows ghosts. In the past, criminals were hung from trees next to crossroads. This is because people thought that if they came back as a ghost, they would be confused by the routes. As a result, the ghost would be unable to leave and haunt them. Their spirits, called gallows ghosts, often appear at crossroads.

Some ghostly folk stay with the same families for hundreds of years. These ghosts may have a favourite bedroom where they sit at the end of the bed! In Denmark, one family ghost looks like a body hanging from a gallows. When the ghost appears, it means someone in the family will die.

GHOSTS OF THE FAMOUS

Many witnesses have reported seeing the ghosts of famous people. Maybe they just want to see a celebrity!

US President Abraham Lincoln was assassinated in 1865. His ghost haunts the White House in Washington, D.C. In the 1930s, Queen Wilhelmina of the Netherlands was staying there. She heard a knock on the door. When she opened it, there stood Lincoln!

GHOSTLY BEINGS

Human ghosts are terrifying enough. Now imagine a ghostly dog, eyes glowing red in the dark, ready to pounce. Watch out for those huge fangs!

Ghost animals are as common as human ghosts. They can be almost any animal you can think of. A ghostly monkey haunts Drumlanrig Castle in Scotland. The ghost of a giant wild horse called the 'White Devil' haunts the deserts of the United States. When it was alive it trampled to death anyone who came near its herd.

The most common ghost animals are black dogs. These often appear to people just before they die. Some of these ghostly hounds have been seen bursting into balls of fire or exploding. Black Shuck is a phantom black hound seen in many parts of England. Arthur Conan Doyle based his famous story, The *Hound of the Baskervilles*, on him.

"Standing over Hugo, and plucking at his throat, there stood a foul thing, a great, black beast, shaped like a hound, yet larger than any hound that ever mortal eye has rested upon. And even as they looked the thing tore the throat out of Hugo Baskerville, on which, as it turned its blazing eyes and dripping jaws upon them, the three shrieked with fear and rode for dear life, still screaming, across the moor."

From *The Hound of the Baskervilles* (1901) by Arthur Conan Doyle.

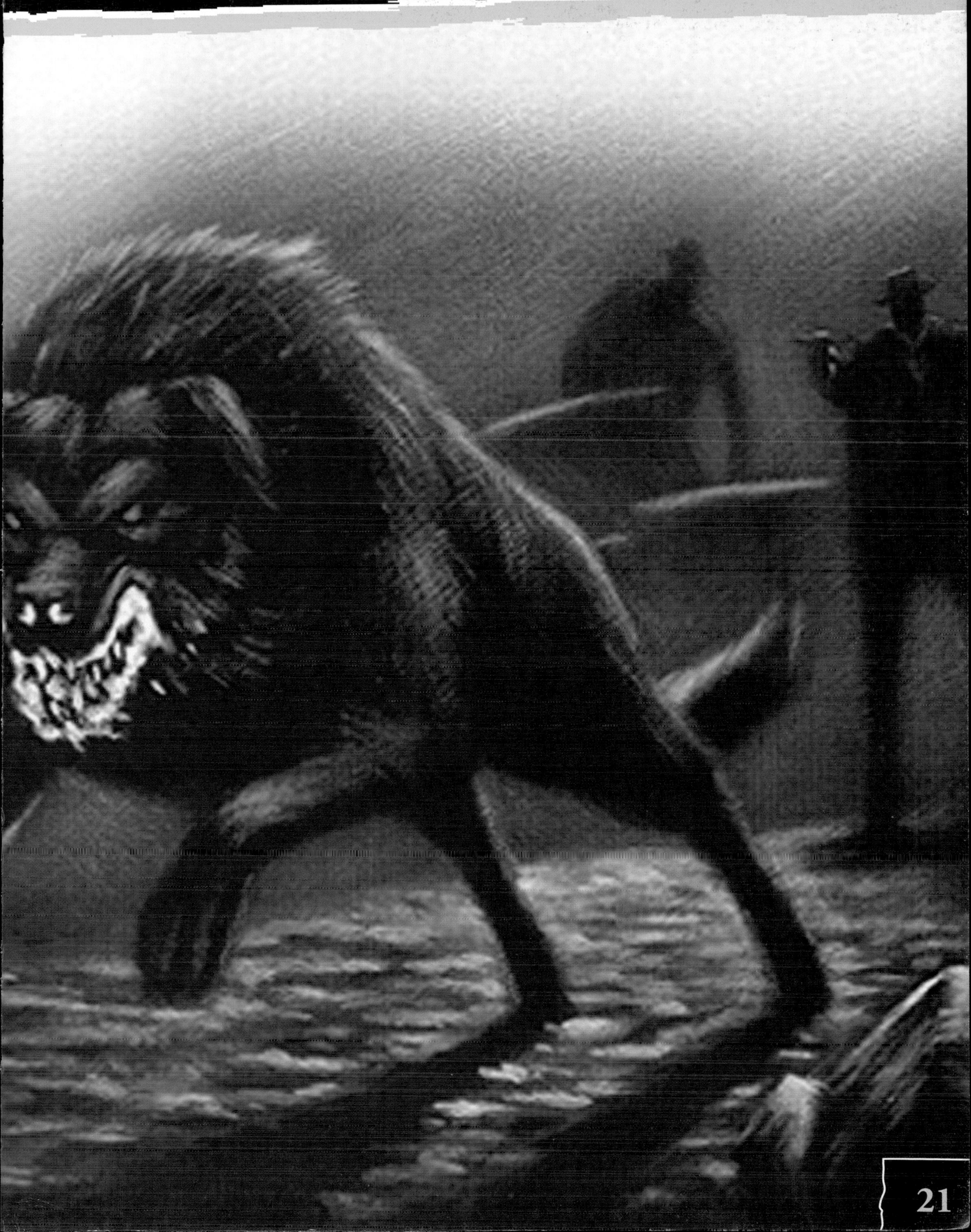

"If it is moonlight, clouds cover over the moon as the phantom train goes by. After the pilot passes, the funeral train itself with flags and streamers rushes past. The track seems covered with a black carpet and the coffin is seen in the centre of the car, while all about it in the air and on the train behind are vast numbers of blue-coated men, some with coffins on their backs."

Description of the Phantom Funeral Train in *The Albany Times*.

PHANTOM OBJECTS

Ghostly trains pull into stations where no track remains. Shadowy ships hover in mid-air. These are phantoms, ghostly objects with a life of their own!

The ghost of wicked Lady Howard travels in a phantom coach made from the bones of her husbands. The skeleton of a dog runs beside the coach on its journey to Okehampton Castle in Devon. Each night the dog picks a blade of grass to take back to Lady Howard's family home. The coach must take this journey until every blade of grass is picked – that is, forever! It is Lady Howard's punishment for murdering her four husbands.

In 1641, a ship called the *Flying Dutchman* tried to sail around the Cape of Good Hope, in Africa. The ship hit rocks during a fierce storm and began to sink. The captain cried, "I will get around the Cape even if I have to keep sailing until Doomsday". His wish came true! This phantom ship still sails the seas, bringing bad luck to all who see it.

THE GHOSTS OF FLIGHT 401

Worldwide, there are stories of ghost planes soaring silently across the night sky. These ghostly planes seem to turn up after tragic air crashes.

In 1972, an Eastern Airlines jet crashed in the Florida Everglades. Soon after, the ghosts of the captain and engineer saved a plane from crashing by warning the crews of danger.

GHOSTS AROUND THE WORLD

It's a party! Special foods are prepared. Red lanterns are hung. There is dancing and singing. Then fires are lit on the path from the graveyard to the house – to help ghosts find their way to the celebrations!

The Obon Festival described above takes place in Japan each year. After three days of celebrations, floating lanterns are dropped into rivers or the sea to guide ghosts back to the spirit world.

In Mexico, ghosts are welcomed into the home during the Day of the Dead festival. People celebrate the dead with colourful sugar skeletons and skulls. They also have big picnics.

In the past, people in Europe and North America tried to keep ghosts away from their home. In ancient Europe, people believed that Hallowe'en was a night when dead spirits left their graves and wandered the Earth. Today, children celebrate Hallowe'en by dressing up and shouting 'trick or treat'.

THE HUNGRY GHOST FESTIVAL

The Chinese believe the gates of Hell open once a year. Hungry ghosts then wander the Earth looking for food. Families leave out food, so the ghosts will bring them good luck.

They also burn paper models, such as houses, cars, TV sets and mobile phones. They believe that these items will help the ghosts live comfortably in the spirit world. They also burn fake money, called Hell Money, so that ghosts will have more cash to spend!

"Peeves smashed lanterns and snuffed out candles, juggled burning torches over the heads of screaming students, caused neatly stacked piles of parchment to topple into fires or out of windows; flooded the second floor when he pulled off all the taps in the bathrooms, dropped a bag of tarantulas in the middle of the Great Hall during breakfast ....."

A description of Peeves the poltergeist from *Harry Potter and the Order of the Phoenix* (2003) by J. K. Rowling.

SPOOKY TALES

You're sitting around a campfire. It's late at night and someone is telling a spine-chilling ghost story. Then – CRACK! There's a sound in the bushes behind you! Would you go and investigate?

Even people who don't really believe in ghosts enjoy spooky stories. Harry Potter's school, Hogwarts, is haunted by over twenty ghosts, including Nearly Headless Nick, grim Bloody Baron and the jolly Fat Friar. The ghost Myrtle sometimes gets flushed out of the castle with the contents of the toilet! These ghosts enjoy a Deathday Party on the anniversaries of their deaths.

Many other famous books and plays also contain ghosts. They appear in the *Goosebumps* horror series written by R.L. Stine. In *A Christmas Carol* by Charles Dickens, three ghosts visit the miserable Scrooge. They encourage him to be more generous and enjoy life. What's the scariest story you know?

FACT OR FICTION?

MOVIE GHOSTS

A teenager walks along a dusty corridor. The lights flicker. The music gets louder. A ghostly hand reaches out from the darkness. The girl lets out a terrified scream – 'Aaaaaargh!' So does the audience!

Ghost movies have been scaring people for over a hundred years. The first horror movie was *The Haunted Castle* (1896) directed by Georges Méliès. Méliès used trapdoors and mirrors to make his ghosts float and vanish.

Since then, special effects have made spooky faces appear, ghosts walk through walls and poltergeists throw objects. As you can see from this picture, *Ghostbusters* (1984) made the most of these effects.

Some ghost movies are based on stories such as *The Legend of Sleepy Hollow* (1999). Other movies are set in the present. In *The Sixth Sense* (1999), a young boy believes he can see and talk to the spirits of the dead.

GOOD OR BAD SPIRITS?

Some movie ghosts are helpful. Others are mean and try to harm or kill people. There are movies about friendly ghosts, like *Casper* (1995). Casper tries hard to make friends with people, but ends up scaring them.

In the movie *The Frighteners* (1996), the hero gets a bump on his head that lets him talk to ghosts. He joins up with three friendly ghosts to track down killer ghosts.

FACT OR FICTION?

DO GHOSTS EXIST?

After hundreds of years of people seeing ghosts, no one has ever been able to really prove that they exist. What do you think?

Nine out of ten ghosts are probably tricks of our imagination. Tired minds mix up real life and dreams. It's easy to see strange things in the dark.

Terrible events put people into a state of shock. They are more likely to imagine things. For example, an awful tsunami hit the Thai island of Phi Phi in early 2005. Afterwards, many people reported the ghost of a woman calling for her lost child.

Can we trust everyone who sees a ghost? In the past, telling ghost stories was a way of keeping strangers away. Often people claiming to speak to spirits are looking for money or fame. Many are shown to be cheats.

FAKE PHOTOS

Some ghost hunters claim they have taken photographs of ghosts. However, many of these have been proven to be fakes.

In the 19th century, photography was new and most people did not understand how cameras worked. For example, when two shots are taken using the same piece of film, the two images sit on top of each other. This is called double exposure. It makes people look shadowy and ghost-like. Try it yourself with a camera that uses film.

GHOST TOWNS

Quiet places can seem spooky, especially deserted buildings. No one lives in the old mining town of Bodie in California any more. It is a ghost town. Walking around it feels strange. We expect to see people but we don't.

Water running below a house can cause creaks and groans. At night, houses cool down, making the walls creak. Pipes make gurgling noises. Books fall off the shelves, creating a sliding sound, a short silence, then a giant clatter! Pets make all sorts of night-time noises.

GLOSSARY & INDEX

Afterlife Where souls travel after death.
Ancestors Members of your family born before you.
Behead To cut off someone's head.
Burial Placing a dead body into a grave.
Cemetery or graveyard A place where bodies are buried.
Corpse A dead body.
Detector A machine that finds things.
Ectoplasm The mysterious material that ghosts are supposedly made of. It can be like a mist or a gooey liquid.
Execute To kill someone as punishment.
Foe An enemy.
Gallows A large wooden frame used for hanging criminals. It was often built at a crossroads.
Ghost town A deserted town.
Haunt A ghost that keeps appearing in the same place is said to haunt that place.

Hoax An attempt to trick people into believing that something false is real.
Hound Another word for a dog, especially a hunting dog.
Malevolent A malevolent spirit is one that wants to hurt or scare people.
Medium Someone who is sensitive to, and may get messages from, ghosts.
Mucus A sticky, slimy substance.
Paranormal This means "beyond normal". It describes anything that we can't explain using science.
Phantom A ghostly figure or object, such as a phantom ship or coach.
Poltergeists A noisy ghost that moves things and makes noises.
Sighting A ghost sighting means an occasion when a ghost has been seen.
Spook/spectre Other words for ghost.
Spooky Strange or scary.